OLD SOULS

The Sages and Mystics of Our World

ALETHEIA LUNA

Copyright

Old Souls: The Sages and Mystics of Our World.

Copyright © Aletheia Luna, 2015

Cover photography "One Tree Hill" by Neil Williamson

ISBN 13: 978-1519546104

All rights reserved. No part of this book may be reproduced or transmitted in any form or by any means, electronic or mechanical, including photocopying, recording, or by any information storage and retrieval system, without permission in writing from the author.

For Sol: friend, teacher, twin flame.

Table of Contents

Preface ix

Introduction xi

Chapter 1 How Can a Soul be "Old"? 1

Chapter 2 The Development of Soulful Maturity 5

Chapter 3 What Does Being an "Old Soul" Mean? 9

Chapter 4 "It's No Big Deal." A Profile of the Old Soul Character 15

Chapter 5 "You Do Your Thing, and I'll Do Mine."
The Old Soul's Relationship with Family 25

Chapter 6 "Just Go With The Flow." The Old Soul's
Relationship with People and the World 33

Chapter 7 Soul Ages, Reincarnation, and Abraham Maslow 39

Chapter 8 "Why Do I Feel Older Than Old?"
The Seven Levels of Feeling Old 49

Chapter 9 Are You a Sage or a Mystic? 55

Chapter 10 "Just Let Me Be." The Old Soul Child 59

Chapter 11 Are You an Awakened Old Soul? 71

Chapter 12 How to Deal with Loneliness,
Emptiness and Disconnection as an Old Soul 77

Chapter 13 What Do Life, Death, Truth and Love Really Mean? 91

Chapter 14 "Old Souls Don't Identify With Labels."
Exploring the Transcendental Soul 95

Conclusion 99

Appendix 101

Sage and Mystic Test 109

Bibliography 115

About the Author 117

Other Books by Aletheia Luna 119

"How old would you be if you didn't know how old you are?"

– Satchel Paige

Preface

Like ancient trees that stand alone on barren landscapes, Old Souls are hard to miss. There is a penetrating intensity to their eyes and a timeworn depth to their being that many say could only be forged through centuries of experience.

It is the Old Soul's unearthliness that makes them natural-born mystics.

It is their innate wisdom that sanctions them as our world's God-given sages.

And it is their unquenchable thirst for truth that ordains them as powerful teachers and beacons of our world's conscious evolution.

Yet despite these gifts and capabilities, Old Souls are like eternal vagabonds, wandering through a world that feels alien and remote. As social anomalies, Old Souls are the quintessential square pegs in our society's round holes. As psychological fringe-dwellers, Old Souls carry around the sensation that this world is not their true home.

What happens when you can see too deep and too much? What happens when the desires, dreams and values of your society no longer hold any interest for you? Such is the life of the old at heart.

Yet, despite this pervading sense of existential displacement, my hope is that this book can be like a refreshing oasis on a hot summer's day. Using the simple, clear and concise information provided in this book, you can discover more about what it means to be an Old Soul, what social and spiritual implications this has on your life, and how to use such a discovery for greater inner growth and healing.

Introduction

*"There is a beautiful thing inside you
that is thousands of years old.
Too old to be captured in poems.
Too old to be loved by everyone.
But loved so very deeply
by a chosen few."*

– Nikita Gill

»

The truth is that I can't really recall ever feeling like one of the rest or "part of the club." For as far back as I can remember I have felt like the sore thumb or black sheep of the pack, never quite fitting in.

Perhaps you can relate to this feeling. Perhaps throughout your life you have stood in a crowd of people and felt like the lonely outsider looking in. Perhaps you have sat down in a room and felt like the eternal foreigner who never quite blends in.

Perhaps at times you have even felt like a world-weary old man or woman gazing at the world with timeworn eyes, despite how young your physical age or appearance is.

If you are like me, you have felt all of these sensations many times before, feeling much older and much more "seasoned" than your physical age reflects. If this is the case, you are inevitably a social outsider. But here is your opportunity to breathe a sigh of relief: I believe there is a very good reason why we experience such misplaced feelings and perceptions in life, and in this book I will show you why. Before that however, I want to briefly share with you a bit about my own story and how this book came to be.

THE OLD PERSON WITHIN

December 2011 was one of the most prophetic months of my life. It was a time when I first met my teacher and future partner, Don Mateo Sol, and was first introduced to the notion of "Old Souls" and later "soulful maturity."

Before that however, life was very grim. Although I had managed to get into university, I was stranded in a very dark period of my life. At that time I lost my lifelong religious faith, my family's respect, my sense of direction, my meaning in life and the last ounce of trust I had in myself. An existential crisis was constantly looming in the background of my life like a hoard of melancholy clouds on a winter's day. Every morning when I woke up it felt as though the ground had been ripped out from underneath me. I remember how depressing it felt to not know what to do with my life or how to find my way again. Life just felt like one big mess that made no sense, and the future felt like a vacant black hole.

So I felt great relief when Sol suddenly emerged from nowhere into the gloomy mists of my life.

Never in my life had I ever found someone who could truly understand me and meet me on the same wavelength. It was as though all of my silent prayers had been miraculously answered out of the blue.

Don Mateo Sol was then – and still is now – a strangely charismatic person. At times he has the quality of a mischievous child: curious, defiant and playful. At others, he has the quality of an old man: pensive, weary and wizened. His words, like his eyes, have a piercing quality that stays with you long after he has left.

Early one morning while we were seated under an old maple we called the "Buddha Tree," Sol said some words that I will never forget. I recall our conversation going something like this:

Me: "I get this strange feeling sometimes – sort of like I'm looking out through the eyes of an old woman ... I don't know. I just don't feel like I belong. I guess I never have."

Sol: "I know what you mean. Since I was young I've always felt as though I could see too deep and too much. That's probably why we get each other so much; we're Old Souls."

Me: "It's a strange feeling ... I look at people around me and think, *Why do you care about this stuff – money, titles, prestige? It's all going to fade; it's all going to die*. It makes me sad because I know they're all going to die unhappy."

The conversation carried on for quite a while, but even though I have forgotten most of its original flow, I still remember the mention of the curious phrase "Old Soul," which has always stayed with me.

Years later, after authoring a number of popular articles on the topic, creating and administering an online group that (to date) consists of over 10,000 self-identified Old Souls, and receiving the stories of hundreds of people who feel "old inside," I have decided to compile my findings in this book.

Chapter 1

How Can a Soul be "Old"?

»

Is there really such a thing as an "Old Soul"? How can this be if time is a relative construct of the human mind? And besides ... aren't souls eternal?

These are only some of the many questions I have come across in my time researching and writing about Old Souls, and all of these questions are very important and valid.

The problems arise when we interpret the phrase "Old Soul" literally rather than *symbolically* or figuratively. The general consensus among people of all religions, spiritual practices and traditions since the dawn of time has been that our souls are immaterial, ageless, changeless and eternal. They represent the essence of who we truly are and they signify the deepest craving many of us possess in life: to be at One with our essential nature. Therefore, it is absurd to think that a soul can really "age," for the phrase is self-contradictory. But that is only if we rationally and literally analyze it.

Instead, being an "Old Soul" refers to something much deeper than its surface meaning. It essentially refers to a *feeling* we carry inside that can only be described using a limited and finite word to encapsulate a vast and indescribable experience. The phrase "Old Soul" is the closest many can come to describing those who feel like they have seen and done it all before, who can see through the lies and illusions of existence, and who experience a tired longing to "return home." The desire to return home is just another figurative expression that reveals the thirst to return back to the Source, God, Oneness, or Soul.

But the question still remains: If some feel "old" inside, why don't others? Furthermore, what does the feeling of being older than your chronological age really *mean* or *point* to?

As Sol wrote in his article entitled "Soulful Energy: Origins of the Soul,"

"What drives one person to pursue material ambitions and momentary pleasures for their entire lives, and another to search for something deeper and more meaningful?

What allows two people to witness the same poignant scene of earthly suffering, but only one of them experience a deep enough "awakening" to completely change their lives?

What makes some people more mature, receptive and compassionate than others?"

He goes on to explain:

"The answer is a greater sensitivity to one's inner wisdom, or a deeper receptivity to one's own soul."

This greater sensitivity and inner receptivity to the depths of one's being can be understood as "Soulful Maturity."

Chapter 2

The Development of Soulful Maturity

»

Some say that we are born again and again into this life as a product of the laws of karma and rebirth. Others say that we choose our bodies, destinies and personalities before we are born in order to further our soul's development.

Whatever the cause of us being here, it is undeniable that some people in life remain perpetually "young at heart" while others remain perpetually "old at heart."

While some people seem to be caught up in the world of the ego, others seem to be irresistibly drawn towards the world of the soul. While some people relentlessly pursue fame, titles, money, properties, lovers and academic accomplishment, others tirelessly seek truth, wisdom, love and freedom beyond the material plane.

How many times, for instance, have you come across people who live for nothing but material status and social stardom?

These people might spend their lives as workaholics, aiming for nothing but "rising through the ranks" in their companies or businesses. Or they might spend their time renovating their houses, constantly upgrading their furnishings, buying the best gadgets, saving up to go on luxurious holidays, and so forth.

On the other hand, you might have come across those few rare people who don't take much interest in worldly attainment or social politics; their focus is not on forming a prestigious name, gathering powerful friends or beautiful lovers, being admired and envied, etc. These people instead are content with their own simple company and their own quiet lives. However, far from being straightforward and simplistic, these philosophical characters seem to constantly be on a "quest" of some sort. This quest is often a spiritual or existential journey that forms the framework for their entire lives.

This essential difference between these two different types of people in life reveals the essence of what Soulful Maturity is.

For some people, the connection that is built to the soul remains like a bud; young, tender and still ready to blossom. For others, the connection that is built to the soul is like a flower; matured, flowered and hardened.

An Old Soul, in this case, is a person who has developed more Soulful Maturity than others. In other words, the connection the Old Soul has built to the soul has opened, flowered and matured. This does not make the Old Soul "better" or "superior" to the younger souls. Instead, it makes them more capable of connecting with the essence of who they truly are beyond their socially conditioned identity.

In essence, the Old Soul finds it easier to connect with the soul because the hole in the ego through which the soul can be glimpsed has widened, whereas for others it remains small and constricted. The reason for this is a mystery, but many theorize that reincarnation has a part to play in this phenomenon. It is said that the more times a soul "returns" to this world through the process of rebirth, the more lessons it learns and thus the "older" and more mature it becomes. We will explore this later in the book.

Chapter 3

What Does Being an "Old Soul" Mean?

»

During my time writing this book, I had the privilege of asking an online group of over 10,000 self-identified Old Souls the question, "What does it mean to be an Old Soul?" The responses I received were fascinating, surprising and varied. However, beneath every layer of response there were a variety of shared characteristics that we will identify afterwards.

Here is a small sample of the responses that I received. My gratitude goes out to those who gave me their permission to include their words in this book:

> "To me an old soul is a soul that has been around for a long time through many, many reincarnations; a soul that recognizes at its core that it is one with the Divine Universe." – Margaret Gardner, California, USA

"An Old Soul is a more aware and conscious soul who has lived many lives and is here for a special purpose. A soul is not really old; because as it is said there is no time in the spiritual realm, so it is just a word used by humans to describe experienced souls." – Gurpreet Singh Matharoo, India

"An Old Soul is a soul that is shackled to its earthen body yet tries to transcend to the heavens, with a thirst for knowledge and wisdom that cannot be satisfied. It is like drinking from the sea. The more you drink, the more you are thirsty." – Ahmed Sameer Ahmed, Colorado, USA

"To me being an Old Soul is being able to enjoy a slow paced journey, getting joy from conversations, honestly sharing different experiences, smiling at the little things, and watching over my fellow travelers whenever they feel lost." – Francesco Costanzo, Italy

"For me, being an Old Soul means being perpetually frustrated with the world. So many people go about their lives chasing things that don't matter, getting angry over trivialities, and they have their priorities completely reversed." – Chance White, Arkansas, USA

"For me an Old Soul is someone who is always seeking to find the answers to the deepest longings of the soul: the perpetual seeker." – Jennifer Floranza Pillarda, Philippines

"Someone who knows true sadness, respects it, but never lets it influence their life." – Whit Jackson, Florida, USA

"An Old Soul is someone who (occasionally) thinks: 'Why? What could I possibly add? Everything has been said and done already.'" – Dimitri Grigorev, Norway

"An Old Soul is to me someone who has been walking the path longer than most, but most importantly has made all the mistakes and learned from all of them. The Old Soul then passes on what was learned." – Thijs Jansen, Netherlands

"I try to describe my experience as an Old Soul in this life as a person whose mind and spirit develops faster than her body can age." – Natalie Elizabeth, Canada

"My whole life has felt like I am living on a poor, barbaric but very beautiful planet. I love it, and I love humans – but this is not my real home." – Brenda Tanner, Texas, USA

"An Old Soul is someone who experiences intense passion in every activity he does. He is overwhelmed with compassion, which makes him attractive to other souls, but he chooses to enjoy his time alone for most parts of his life." – Collins B-Lai, Kenya, Africa

"I think of an Old Soul as one who has been here many times before. There is a depth in their eyes, a depth of knowledge, a depth of wisdom, a depth of knowing." – Sherry Coté, Connecticut, USA

Which of these reflections resonated with you the most? As we can see, how people define the Old Soul varies across different personalities, nationalities and backgrounds, but all of the answers reveal similar threads of thought and feeling. These similarities can be narrowed down to the following observations:

1. Old Souls are contemplative and philosophical people.
2. Old Souls are able to see the bigger picture.
3. Old Souls are drawn to knowledge, wisdom and truth.
4. Old Souls are innately spiritual people.

5. Old Souls are emotionally and psychologically mature.

Even though they are said to compose 10–15% of the population of the world (it is impossible to be precise), up until the publication of this book Old Souls have rarely been examined or written about in depth.

So here is your invitation: If you're curious to learn more about Old Souls – either because you personally identify as one or because you have one in your life right now – I welcome you to travel with me through the rest of these pages in the spirit of inquiry.

Chapter 4

"It's No Big Deal." A Profile of the Old Soul Character

»

Although we have briefly touched on what it means to be an Old Soul in the previous chapter, it is essential for us to further elaborate on the Old Soul temperament to gain a deeper, more nuanced understanding of *who* they are. For example, what does the Old Soul cherish and value, dislike and avoid, and feel about the person they are? What can be said about their tastes, aspirations and goals in life?

You will find all of this information in this chapter, plus more.

1) LIKES AND PREDISPOSITIONS

A lot can be said about the Old Soul's preferences in life.

Nearly all of the collective knowledge and experience that I've gathered on this topic has shown that the basic desire of the Old Soul is *personal and spiritual fulfillment*, whether that be through love, occupation or intellectual realization. If you're an Old Soul, you will find that you tend to:

- Prefer mental and/or emotional satisfaction when working, rather than fame or success
- Value wisdom, knowledge and understanding both in yourself and others
- Gravitate towards philosophical, humanitarian or artistic pursuits
- Be attracted to philosophy, mysticism, metaphysics and the occult as ways of reaching personal fulfillment
- Prefer the company of a few like-minded people, or else prefer habitual solitude
- Prefer pacifism to drama, and minimalism to consumerism
- Have old-fashioned tastes (e.g., old movies, old people, old objects, old music, etc.)

Because the Old Soul tends to see very few things on the physical plane as being very much of "a big deal," they like focusing their energy towards spiritually and emotionally rewarding pursuits.

II) DISLIKES AND DISINCLINATIONS

The Old Soul finds that they never truly despise anything in life. Rather, they tend to have a dislike for:

- Ignorant and/or foolish behavior
- The company of dramatic and frantic people
- Too many time-consuming social connections
- Unnecessary pressures, demands and expectations
- Too many material attachments
- General affairs of the world, e.g., politics, debates, careers, money, etc.
- Gossip and other trivialities

Essentially, anything too worldly, too short-sighted or too mentally and emotionally exhausting is shunned by the Old Soul.

Like an old person, the Old Soul is easily tired by pressure, tension and conflict. To them, the matters of everyday life are unsurprising, commonplace and inconsequential in the greater scheme of things.

III) PERSONAL TRIBULATIONS

"This world is not my home. I'm just a-passin' through.
My treasures are laid up somewhere beyond the blue.
The angels beckon me from heaven's open door,
And I can't feel at home in this world anymore."
– Albert E. Brumley

The Old Soul, however, is not free from problems, issues and burdens. Just like everyone else, Old Souls are not immune to the afflictions of everyday life.

The biggest issue for the Old Soul isn't whether he can pay the rent, get a job promotion or retrieve the affection of a lost lover. Rather, his greatest tribulation has to do with *existence*.

It's not uncommon for the Old Soul to experience some measure of depression, apathy or existential lethargy when it comes to living everyday life. After all, if physical existence loses its star-spangled gleam, and everyday affairs lose their burning importance what is the point of living a dull life?

In this instance, the Old Soul who lacks a fundamental meaning, hobby or passion falls into a state of existential crisis.

If the everyday earthly issues that the Old Soul experiences genuinely fail to dominate or hijack their lives – as they do with others – what is there worth fighting for? If other people are predictable and habitually create havoc, what's the point of existing in such a burdensome society? If everything is passing by, what is the point of becoming attached to anything?

Innately, the Old Soul carries a sense of world-weariness as he stands on the outside, looking in. As an observer, the Old Soul, like the Steppenwolf, feels an all-pervading sense of alienation. He is the ultimate outsider who is both *in* the world but not quite *of* the world at the same time.

This sense of continual remoteness from the world can lead to a constant sense of loneliness and unhappiness. Inevitably, this can lead to mental health issues such as depression. But that's not to say that *all* depressed people are necessarily Old Souls. In addition to the Old Soul's lack of interest in daily affairs, there can also, at times, be a struggle with existential apathy or indifference. After all, since the path towards peace is to "live and let live," what's the point of doing anything?

"*Vanitas vanitatum!*"

Since all that is said and done is tiresome and transient, what's the point of participating in life?

"*Been there, done that!*"

Life can be seen as "a drag" and somewhat pointless from the perspective of an Old Soul. At times, existence can even be perceived as one big *Divine Comedy*. The drives, motivations, and behaviors of other people are so well understood that they're almost comical at times, and at other times wearisome and futile.

But all is not doom and gloom for the Old Soul. When living with meaning and a sense of purpose, especially in the field of teaching, Old Souls emanate a sense of penetrating sensitivity and discernment that few others can match.

Additionally, the Old Soul rarely sees anything as "senseless" – *tedious* perhaps, but never without meaning. In the Old Soul's holistic perception of the self as being part of the bigger picture, *everything has a reason*. Therefore, the Old Soul strives to be at peace with the trials and tribulations in his life. In this respect, his goal is to remain steadfast in his inner sanctuary of calm. To achieve such peace and composure amid the troubles of life is to become a true Spiritual Master.

IV) INNER TRIUMPHS

Deep underneath the Old Soul's calm exterior lies a burning desire to attain wisdom, understanding and universal truth. In essence, the Old Soul's thirst for deep spiritual insight is his greatest crowning glory.

In his quest for spiritual progression, the Old Soul can find himself deconstructing the world around him and seeing through many of the lies and illusions created through various traditions, beliefs and institutions. Perhaps it was the Old Soul's first feelings of being an alien in a world that doesn't feel like home that set him on his path.

Whatever the cause, the Old Soul finds himself slowly awakening to the beauty and interconnectedness of life through his pursuit of truth. "Everything is connected" was probably a phrase first coined by an Old Soul.

Among the Old Soul's greatest achievements in life is his ability to live with inner peace, even amid the troubles of existence. As all is passing, the Old Soul understands the importance of non-attachment to physical and immaterial things. His composure amongst the chaos of life is precisely what makes him an excellent Spiritual Teacher.

As materialism and the delusions of physical existence lose their grip, the Old Soul becomes less and less interested in everyday life, and more interested in the world of the spirit.

Similarly, as the Old Soul learns not to react or become attached to his transitory thoughts and feelings, he learns to simply observe life as it is.

No longer is he one amongst many, but instead One *with* many. Thus, the Old Soul's great triumph in life is his progressive transcendence of the Ego Self to a mortal glimpse into the Universal Self. Because of this, it's not unusual for the Old Soul to appear "otherworldly" and "strange," as though he is lit up from within, or as though he has attained some small measure of *enlightenment*.

V) ODD ABILITIES

In a survey conducted within my group of almost 10,000 self-identifying Old Souls online, well over 90% of the respondents said their Myer Briggs Type Indicator (MBTI) personality scores indicated they were intuitive ("N") types of people. Most identified as either INFJ, INFP, INTJ or INTP types.

Unsurprisingly, these results perfectly reflect the spiritual nature of Old Souls, who use their highly developed intuitive abilities to navigate through life.

After all, the Old Soul is not ruled simply by the conscious mind, which creates cynicism and dryness, or the unconscious mind, which creates instinctual chaos. Rather, he operates calmly in both spheres.

Perhaps it's this balance that creates so many of the odd and otherworldly experiences in the Old Soul's lifetime. In fact, it's quite common for the Old Soul to experience what many people would refer to as "new age phenomena." These vast and varied experiences range from sensations as commonplace as experiencing vivid and repeated déjà vu to other sensations as complex as precognition – the foreseeing of an event or series of events in a dream which later transpire in real life.

Whether these experiences offer evidence of higher evolutionary brain functioning or brief glimpses into a deeper Universal Mind continues to be a mystery. In any case, the Old Soul is acutely aware of his strange gifts, sometimes even from early childhood.

It's also not uncommon for Old Souls to develop some level of *clairvoyance* or *sixth sense* in their lifetimes.

This is not necessarily the psychic ability to predict events in the future – although that is not beyond the Old Soul – but rather the ability to intuitively and perceptively understand the people around them at a very profound level. This is often referred to as "seeing through people." In other words, this is the ability to see beyond the external masks, pretentions and affectations of a person or group of people to see into their deeper hidden characters, thoughts, feelings and motives. For this reason, it's very hard to fool the Old Soul, who can easily differentiate the charlatan from the truth teller, the malicious from the kind-hearted, the unstable from the balanced, and the shallow man from the thoughtful man.

Additionally, many Old Souls have claimed to have *empathic* abilities that allow them to intuitively *feel* the emotions of others. The *Empath* is often said to have such a great degree of *empathy* that they can literally feel what others feel; therefore, they intuitively know many of the yearnings, sensitivities, tastes and even thought patterns of the people they're around.

This is often referred to as the ability to "feel other people's energy" and is thought of as both a blessing and a curse.

On one hand, the Empath is able to intuitively help those in need since they have the ability to understand the people around them to a very deep degree. On the other hand, the Empath is often weighed down and overwhelmed by emotions, which can create physical and psychological disharmony, and even sickness in the body. This intense connection to the emotional world is a defining characteristic of feeling-orientated Old Souls, who are excellent counselors and emotional strongholds to those around them.

However, this is not to say that *all* spiritually gifted people are necessarily Old Souls, just as not all Old Souls are necessarily spiritually gifted. The Old Soul simply experiences a greater connection to the subconscious mind, which sometimes results in odd abilities and seemingly supernatural gifts.

Chapter 5

"You Do Your Thing, and I'll Do Mine." The Old Soul's Relationship with Family

»

Few really understand the Old Soul in entirety. Those who do somewhat understand their inner workings usually tend to be family members, partners or very close friends. Rarely does the Old Soul wear his heart on his sleeve.

So what can be said about the Old Soul and family? What are their feelings about romance, sex, children and in-laws?

I) RELATIONSHIPS

Although Old Souls tends to be "lone wolves" by nature, they often yearn to find one person whom they can share all of their thoughts, insights and outlooks on life with. Usually, when it comes to relationships, Old Souls tend to wait patiently for their Soul Mate or Twin Flame to emerge.

The Old Soul rarely tends to actively seek lovers out. In this regard, their philosophy tends to be: "If it's meant to be, let it be." However, this is not to say that Old Souls are indifferent to romantic companionship. They simply trust that when the time is right, the Universe, God or destiny will introduce the right person into their lives.

Usually, the Old Soul tends to be very careful when it comes to intimate involvement with another person. They prefer to avoid the drama that comes with bonding with too many people at one time. For this reason, the Old Soul rarely sleeps around or sees more than one person at a time.

Monogamy tends to be the preferred lifestyle of the Old Soul, not because it's socially acceptable, but because it's the least riddled with complications. Besides, it's quite unusual for the Old Soul to relate to more than two or three people deeply during their lifetimes.

When the Old Soul *is* united with another person, however, they proceed with care and caution.

For a relationship to be successful with an Old Soul, one must be able to connect to them on the profoundest of levels. Love cannot simply be a lustful affair but must be an experience filled with depth and spiritual connection. The Old Soul rarely tolerates superficial entanglements based on surface similarities. Therefore, they tend to fall in love with the *inner character* of a person first, rather than their exterior charm. The money, physical appearance and social popularity of a person rarely interest the Old

Soul, who chooses to focus on the inner qualities of the soul that never fade away.

As for sex, the Old Soul is usually adept but lacks a fundamental interest in physical pleasure, although they still enjoy it. Old Souls certainly possess libidos, but they are not controlled or driven by them to seek out frequent sexual encounters.

Romantically, the Old Soul is usually considered a "gentleman" or "lady," with a rather whimsical and antique taste in sensuality. Writing poetry and songs, cutting off locks of hair, and giving away symbolic pieces of jewelry are quite characteristic of the Old Soul's tastes in romanticism.

As for sexual preference, the Old Soul is not necessarily *innately* heterosexual. Although society dictates that the proper person to love is one of the opposite sex, Old Souls can find themselves attracted to members of their own gender or inter-genders. Rarely are they deterred by the "law of man" in these matters. For this reason, the Old Soul rarely discriminates when it comes to emotional, mental and psychological compatibility.

Additionally, "male" and "female" roles are usually seen as social constructs that the Old Soul is not interested in living by. Thus, the Old Soul can sometimes be androgynous in appearance and behavior. A male could just as easily be sensitive like a female, as a female could just as easily be robust like a male. The Old Soul is not interested in playing the game of "machismo man" or "helpless woman."

On the other hand, the Old Soul easily fits the role of the quintessential Soul Mate. Having a large unconscious repository of insight, understanding and possible experience from past lives, the Old Soul tends to be gifted in sustaining and maintaining relationships.

They are regarded by their lovers as excellent teachers, companions and nurturers. The Old Soul as a Soul Mate understands and accepts the needs, desires and quirks of his lover, knowing that the basic ingredients of long-lasting unions are honesty, intimacy, trust, and emotional and psychological vulnerability. Thus the Old Soul is rarely prone to controlling, abusive or deceptive behaviors in intimate relationships. They really can be said to truly understand their partners, inside and out.

II) CHILDREN

So what can be said about Old Souls and children? Unsurprisingly, the majority of Old Souls make quite lenient and liberal parents. While some are eager to raise children – usually to satisfy their desires to teach and impart wisdom – other Old Souls tend to be indifferent to child rearing, usually because of their lack of energy.

When children do come along, the Old Soul ensures that their child is as free to pursue whatever they desire as possible.

Remembering their own childhood, the Old Soul is intimately aware of their child's need to be freely expressive and to have parents who are nonjudgmental and non-intrusive. Therefore, they are rarely the dominating and controlling parents so often seen in society. In fact, they can even be perceived as "lazy" when it comes to parenting by other people. This could be due to the fact that Old Soul parents lack the frenzy and hysteria many other parents have, preferring to play a passive role in the development of their child instead.

"Live and let live" is the Old Soul's motto when it comes to parenting. There is no use in sheltering a child from the world out of fear, or crushing his wild dreams and strange quirks out of social obligation.

Unfortunately, onlookers often criticize the Old Soul as being "neglectful" and even "hippy" or "libertine" in these situations. Luckily, this rarely fazes the Old Soul; they know what is best for their child, not out of pop psychology parenting manuals but out of wisdom and understanding.

On the other hand, the Old Soul parent is rarely disliked or criticized by their children.

Occasionally, the Old Soul parent might be thought of as eccentric by their offspring, but in general they are appreciated for their calmness, clemency and tolerance.

Above all, children of the Old Soul cherish the wise counsel frequently given, and they develop close bonds that can often last a lifetime with their parent or parents. The almost "psychic connection" present between Old Souls and their children is so strong that it's usually not very difficult for them to ascertain what their child is feeling or even hiding.

III) EXTENDED FAMILY

Mother, father, siblings, aunts, uncles, grandparents, get-togethers, family feuds ... what can be said about the Old Soul's relationship with extended family members?

As with everything, the Old Soul approaches family with a casual, if not detached, attitude. "They can do their thing while I do mine," is the attitude usually held towards family drama, which the Old Soul is not usually one to take part in.

Somehow always on the outskirts quietly looking in, the Old Soul cares about his or her family but does so without becoming too attached to them or their problems. This is not to say that the Old Soul doesn't try to help at all. If anything, they gladly play the part of counselor or adviser to their family members in times of strife.

Because of the Old Soul's ability to go right to the heart of every matter, they are usually the first ones confided in when it comes to household politics.

Although Old Souls can be disliked for their seemingly distant and blasé attitude towards family, they are appreciated for their calming and stabilizing presence and for their penchant for offering good advice, just as they are in close friendships.

After "leaving the nest," so to speak, it's not uncommon for the Old Soul to keep a healthy distance from their families. Being solitary and contemplative people by nature, Old Souls need their own space to thrive and pursue what they love best. In this sense,

Old Souls can be said to have a distinct hedonistic vibe about their characters as they are devoted to pleasure.

Although they love their families, they prefer mellow and relaxed ways of life like old people. Feeling internally retired already from the wiles of the world, the Old Soul lacks the energy and interest to partake in bickering, tension and emotional rollercoasters. As usual, they like observing from a distance and approaching when the waters are calm.

Chapter 6

"Just Go With The Flow." The Old Soul's Relationship with People and the World

»

If you're an Old Soul or are still learning about the Old Soul in your life, it will be apparent by now that the Old Soul displays very unconventional, eccentric and unorthodox attitudes about the world. In this chapter, we'll build on this by exploring the Old Soul's perceptions of education, work, religion and politics.

I) EDUCATION AND CAREER

"Why should we be taught about life when life *is* the school?" is a good way of defining the Old Soul's perceptions towards education.

When it comes to school and college education, the Old Soul is varied in approach.

As a child, the Old Soul was either the diligent and intense student who befriended all the teachers or the rebellious and precocious child who was extremely inquisitive yet easily bored by the stiff curriculum he was forced to study by his teachers. Sometimes, he was even a mix of the two.

Growing up, the Old Soul doesn't see diplomas, degrees, PhDs or other qualifications as possessing much importance or value. If anything, a college or university education is a means towards an end, that is, to further their life purpose or Universal understanding. Respectable and elite careers are of no interest to the Old Soul, who is much too tired to join in with the "my house is bigger than your house" games of society.

If the Old Soul has to work, any job will usually do. It's very uncommon to find Old Souls in prestigious careers, unless they have some higher purpose at play behind the scenes. On the other hand, it's very common for the Old Soul to drop out of educational institutions as they are able to see through the Almighty Career Ploy at a young age.

In fact, many Old Souls don't get college or university educations at all. To them, self-education is of much more worth and value than four years in higher education.

Like the quintessential old person, the Old Soul can often be found reading a book quietly and contentedly. The world is so vast with oceans full of knowledge that trapping yourself within the walls of an institution which forces you to study a single area for four or more years seems quite ludicrous.

For this reason, the Old Soul is more inclined to be a lifelong learner, or *autodidact,* who constantly feeds his thirst for insight through his own persistent efforts.

His learning has not been forced into him through education or learned out of obligation but has been absorbed out of curiosity and personal choice. Perhaps this is one of the main reasons why the Old Soul has such boundless repositories of knowledge when others do not.

He has learned to preserve a yearning for education and thus a heightened awareness and understanding of the Self and Universe, while others have been drowned in "higher education," becoming nauseated at the thought of any further "learning."

To the mind that has been chewed up and spat out by the institutional approach to education, the Old Soul is a very strange whack job indeed. *"Why continue the agony of education?"* society is prone to ponder. *"Are they masochistic or something?"*

Fortunately for the Old Soul, education is something very personal and something to quietly revel in. The Old Soul's individualistic approach to education also tends to give him a bad name. Because of his lack of interest in money or status, the Old Soul can often be thought of as "lazy" and as a bit of a "kook." It's very unsettling for the institutionalized mind to observe someone with so much indifference towards careers and certifications live his life with perfect equanimity. *Could it be true that riches don't make the man after all?*

Indeed, the less material possessions the Old Soul has, the better. Why work hard to make a career, pay off debt, and buy more things when you don't want *things* in the first place!

II) POLITICS AND RELIGION

There's a reason why politics and religion are the two most important topics to keep out of healthy, cordial conversations: they stir up more ego rivalry and worldwide chaos than anything known to man. It's precisely because of this reason that the Old Soul prefers to stay far away from such topics in daily life.

In these matters, the Old Soul is not one to necessarily *fight* or want to *change* the pandemonium caused by differing beliefs, ideals or perspectives. "Let them fight their own fights" is an appropriate philosophy held by the Old Soul, who is much too relaxed to go out on noble crusades to change anything – not that there's anything wrong with that. The Old Soul, however, simply doesn't have the "young, energetic blood" that others have, even when young.

When it comes to politics in particular, the Old Soul rarely chooses one "wing" or "party." In all truth, the Old Soul rarely sees politics as part of his broader life purpose. "

The path of fulfillment doesn't lie in fanatically following one political party," the Old Soul is prone to reason. As one political party drifts into power, another one drifts out of power.

And so life continues with its constant ebb and flow of change. If anything can be said about the Old Soul and politics, it is that they tend to be pacifists or peacemakers – but even this they aren't really that militant about.

On the other hand, the Old Soul does tend to be religiously inclined, although not at all diehard. If the Old Soul *does* align with a set of religious beliefs, he will be discreet and respectful of other's varying beliefs. Fundamentalism, activism and fanaticism are not at all what define the Old Soul's approach to religion. If anything, religion is simply an outlet for spiritual expression or direction, and plays a very passive role in the Old Soul's quest for Unity and fulfillment.

In this area, like many others, the Old Soul is stereotyped as being somewhat eccentric and offbeat. This is because the Old Soul tends to live by the Religion of the Universe, or in other words, an intricately woven patchwork of truths formed by various religious, philosophical and mystical writings.

For instance, it's not unusual for the Old Soul to piece together a cosmic understanding of existence using Buddhist and Sufi teachings, combined with the writings of Nietzsche, Krishnamurti and Kahlil Gibran – and continue to build upon his understanding with more perspectives throughout life.

All in all, the Old Soul's religion is one of love, one of understanding, one of forgiveness and one of non-attachment. Fortunately for the rest of the world, it's not one of "I'm right and you're wrong" or "you're either good or bad, righteous or evil." For this reason, the Old Soul never preaches his personal religion as one of absolute, impervious truth. If he is to teach – which he typically feels drawn to do at one time or another – he merely delivers to those willing to hear what he has learned in his time on earth and possibly his past lives of experience.

The Younger Soul who listens to the Older Soul's message can often misunderstand and even misuse the Older Soul's teachings; nevertheless, the Older Soul merely functions as a messenger to point to a higher truth.

Intuitively, the Old Soul knows that life is not as clear-cut or black-and-white as organized religions tend to make it sound, nor is life meant to be lived in fear of punishment. Rather, the Old Soul strives to make peace with the uncertainty of life and death.

After all, you can fall in love with the mystery, but you can't fall in love with the explanation.

Chapter 7

Soul Ages, Reincarnation, and Abraham Maslow

»

Now that you have developed a well-rounded understanding of the Old Soul temperament, *why exactly* are you (or the one you love) an Old Soul? Why do you feel like an alien, wandering through a world that doesn't really feel like your home? Why are you so different from the people around you? And why do you seem to possess a hidden reservoir of wisdom and understanding inside of you that other people don't seem to have?

What on earth is going on here?

Understanding why we are born the way we are is perhaps the single most important key to gaining true self-knowledge and self-acceptance.

The pressing questions here are: why don't you have a burning interest in career progression, money or social status like everyone else?

Why does the thought of getting a 9 to 5 office job with a big house, mortgage, two cars, a dog and multiple children make you deeply despair?

It's easy for the Old Soul to feel deviant and odd when it comes to these everyday matters. The Old Soul isn't one to follow the beat of society's drum, after all. Their innate thirst for self-actualization and self-fulfillment propels them into alternative lifestyles, or at the very least contributes to their longing for deeper ways of living.

But at the end of the day, Old Souls seek quiet and mellow lives, albeit on their own unique terms.

REINCARNATION OR SIMPLY TEMPERAMENT?

A lot of speculation surrounds why exactly people feel so old inside, even if they may not have lived very long. Is the experience of being an Old Soul a matter of simply nature and nurture, or does it have far greater spiritual or religious implications?

A lot of evidence, for instance, has shown that intelligence can be inherited, which leads to the question: Can wisdom be inherited as well – if not from parents, then from grandparents?

Epigenetics, also loosely known as *Cellular Memory*, is the theory that non-genetic information (such as memories, personalities, and tastes) can be inherited. Could the insight, knowledge and wisdom possessed by Old Souls be the product of generations of inherited experience? Is this the reason why we feel so old inside – a culmination of genetic memory?

After all, it's not an uncommon experience in society to be told that we look exactly like our great-great grandmother, have the precise same character as our great uncle Bob, or have an eerie predilection for pickled onions just like our great-grandfather Joe.

Perhaps, after all, this is why we're so old in heart, mind and soul. Maybe we're simply the genetic conglomeration of our ancestors.

Or maybe not.

A more common explanation for the feeling of being old in soul is tied up in Buddhist and Hindu ideas of reincarnation, or *metempsychosis*. Interestingly, this is most likely where the origin of the phrase "Old Soul" came from in the first place.

Reincarnation, the spiritual notion that the soul of a person is reborn into another individual after death, may be the key to understanding why some feel so old while others feel so young. The most popularly accepted explanation of the Old Soul temperament is linked to a modern *soul ages* reincarnation theory (please see the Bibliography section for more information). This theory states that there are five different soul ages, according to how many past lives an individual has lived. In a nut shell, Old Souls are said to be *the most advanced* in the cycle of reincarnation, paying off the last dregs of Karma that they have incurred in past lifetimes for final liberation. Thus, they occupy the final level in the soul ages theory.

Additionally, four other *soul types* are present in this reincarnational flow. These are the:

1. Infant Souls

This soul type is characterized by a childlike, playful, wild and primitive approach to life.

Like infants, they lack understanding of the basic rules of existence, often being perceived as ignorant, foolish and gullible.

Because they have not learned any lessons from past lives, newly entering the process of reincarnation, Infant Souls are primarily concerned with basic survival needs such as comfort and safety. Their mental focus is predominantly external.

2. Baby Souls

This soul type is characterized by a *naïve*, guileless and black-and-white approach to life. Having freshly entered the reincarnation cycle, Baby Souls have learned the basics of the world in their infant stage and now crave to create order in life's chaos.

Striving to live a civilized and orderly life, Baby Souls tend to focus on tradition, religion, morality and discipline as ways of instituting stability. Common mentalities held by Baby Souls are defined by the notions of "us and them," "good and bad," and "right and wrong."

3. Young Souls

The Young Soul can be defined by an ambitious, self-determined and competitive approach to life. Having lived by other's rules in the previous reincarnation stage, Young Souls now seek to create their own individualistic lives. Like teenagers, Young Souls are mostly motivated by status and prestige, and their focus is primarily on wealth, recognition and independence.

4. Mature Souls

The Mature Soul is defined by a sensitive, introspective and inquisitive approach to life. Unlike Young Souls, Mature Souls place more importance on building and optimizing relationships with other people than on material gain or status.

In this stage of development, the Mature Soul – sensitive to life's complexities – seeks to understand as well as to make meaning out of the life they've been given. This soul's stage is marked by increased open-mindedness to life yet a lot of strenuous self-discovery and psychological tension.

REINCARNATION EVIDENCE

So could Old Souls be the last piece in this cosmic jigsaw puzzle?

After all, there has been a lot of evidence that has shown that the reincarnation of souls could indeed be true. Handwriting analysis, birthmark and birth defect analysis, as well as past life hypnotic regression and the spontaneous recall and special knowledge of previous lifetimes held by children all over the world has made the *soul ages* theory more plausible.

For instance, in one case documented by researcher Carol Bowman in her book *Children's Past Lives*, an 18-month-old little girl named Elspeth showed clear signs of having "been here before." Elspeth, who had never previously spoken a complete sentence, spoke up to her mother one evening as she was being bathed.

"I'm going to take my vows," she said. Her mother, shocked, asked her what she meant by such a strange statement.

"I'm not Elspeth now," the little girl said. "I'm Rose, but I'm going to be Sister Teresa Gregory." Later, she described her nun's habit and the daily chores she would undertake at the convent in detail to her bewildered mother.

This is just one of thousands of stories documented all throughout history that might point to the legitimacy of reincarnation.

Another example that may point to the validity of the soul ages theory lies in the discoveries of past life therapist Nicola Dexter. Dexter, who places her patients under deep medical hypnosis, has uncovered a number of illnesses and ailments in some of her patients that directly relate back to proposed traumatic past life experiences.

Dexter uncovered cases where, for instance, a man who feared razors found that the cause of his anxiety was rooted in a past life experience of having his hand chopped off with a sword as a punishment for chopping off someone else's fingers.

Other cases cited by Dexter include, for example, a man who discovered that the root of his obsession for putting out cigarettes came from a past life experience of being burned to death in a fire caused by a cigarette. Another person discovered that their fear of indoor heights stemmed from a past life experience of being killed accidentally when slipping and falling to the ground while carving the ceiling of a church.

Now, you may be thinking, *This is all fine and good ... but can the soul age's theory be further supported?* Interestingly, the famous psychologist Abraham Maslow might have something to say about this.

THE MASLOW CONNECTION

In 1943 Abraham Maslow proposed that people were motivated by five different needs and that these needs formed the basis of existence. These days, Maslow's hierarchy of needs forms an important part of the framework for many sociological and psychological studies of human nature. But of what importance is that to Old Souls?

Intriguingly, Maslow's widely accepted theory of human needs almost *perfectly* mimics the soul ages theory and can very well form a relevant psychological foundation of proof. Let's take a closer look at Maslow's hierarchy of needs:

Level 5 of Maslow's Hierarchy: Self-Actualization
Needs: Self-fulfillment and realization of one's potential
Reminiscent of: The Old Soul

Level 4 of Maslow's Hierarchy: Self-Esteem
Needs: Recognition, respect and achievement
Reminiscent of: The Young Soul

Level 3 of Maslow's Hierarchy: Belonging
Needs: Friendship, sexual relationships and family
Reminiscent of: The Mature Soul

Level 2 of Maslow's Hierarchy: Safety
Needs: Protection, law, order and stability
Reminiscent of: The Baby Soul

Level 1 of Maslow's Hierarchy: Physiological
Needs: Air, food, shelter, water, warmth and sleep
Reminiscent of: The Infant Soul

As we can see, Maslow's hierarchy mimics the needs of each soul age almost perfectly. Level 1 of Maslow's hierarchy of needs, for instance, perfectly reflects the drives of the Infant Soul, and Level 2 of the hierarchy thoroughly encapsulates the Baby Soul's desires for safety and order.

Interestingly, Maslow puts self-esteem – the fundamental need of the Young Soul – above the need for interpersonal belonging, as needed by the Mature Soul. However, Maslow did note that his hierarchal order of needs wasn't always necessarily restricted to a rigid progression. Nevertheless, level 5 of the hierarchy of needs is said to be the highest need a human can aspire to: self-actualization. This reflects all too well the profoundest need of the Old Soul.

In Maslow's own words, self-actualization "refers to the desire for self-fulfillment, namely, to the tendency for [a person] to become actualized in what [they are] potentially" (1943).

Maslow also believed that in order to truly understand the need for self-actualization, one needed to not only achieve all prior needs but also to master them.

Sound at all similar to the soul ages theory to you? Maslow's analysis of the self-actualized person in his book *Motivation and Personality* (1970) is also strikingly similar to the Old Soul's intrinsic nature.

Below is a list of the characteristics that Maslow proposed belong to the self-actualized person.

See if you can spot the similarities between these characteristics and those shared by Old Souls.

According to Maslow, the self-actualized person:

- Is able to tolerate uncertainty
- Accepts themselves and other people as they are
- Is resistant to enculturation (or the acquisition of the traits and norms of a culture)
- Possesses a democratic attitude
- Is concerned for the welfare of humanity
- Is highly creative
- Needs privacy and solitude
- Deeply appreciates basic life experiences
- Has strong moral/ethical standards
- Can look at life objectively

- Has "peak experiences" (or, in other words, the experience of euphoria, interconnectedness and ego-transcendence)
- Establishes a few deep interpersonal relationships with people

So the question now remains to be answered: Are Old Souls the result of previous lifetimes of learning and experience encapsulated in the body of a single person? And does Maslow's theory support that?

Only you can answer that. Just as beauty is in the eye of the beholder, so too is *meaning* in the eye of the beholder.

Whether the experience of being an Old Soul is the result of temperament and genetic memory or reincarnation and rebirth is your intuitive decision to make.

Chapter 8

"Why Do I Feel Older Than Old?" The Seven Levels of Feeling Old

»

I have heard a variety of puzzling questions materialize while researching people who feel old inside. These questions sound something like this: "Why do I feel *older* than old?" "Is there such a thing as an *Ancient* Soul?" "Why do I enjoy the company of more immature people, even though I'm an Old Soul?" "Why do I still struggle with psychological issues even though I feel like an old woman/man inside?"

How can a person, curious and in search of self-understanding, answer these difficult questions about themselves? Fortunately, there may be one explanation for all of this confounding inner confusion. Just as everything exists in a variety of levels and degrees, it can be said that the Old Soul does as well. Just as animals, plants and human beings go through their own internal and external evolutionary transformations, it can be said that the Old Soul does too.

According to a variety of works linked with the soul ages theory, our souls undergo *seven different levels* of evolution. Think of this as a slow process of "breaking in" to each soul age, and getting used to their new perceptions and perspectives. With seven levels of evolution occurring in each soul age, this means that we can experience a possible 35 levels of perception before we're released from the physical plane.

So what defines these levels, and which one could you – or the one you love – potentially inhabit right now?

LEVEL ONE – THE "TRANSITORY STAGE"

In this level, a person takes a tentative dip into the new waters of consciousness. A level one Old Soul spends two-thirds of their time as a Mature Soul and the other third exploring the world of the Old Soul.

This is called the Transitory Stage because they're only just beginning to learn and adapt to the Old Soul perspective.

Understandably, this is a time of uneasiness as their habitual way of perceiving the world is being slowly replaced with a new, alien perspective.

Examples: *Carlos Castaneda, Igor Stravinsky, Tommy Lee Jones*

LEVEL TWO – THE "COMPARE AND CONTRAST STAGE"

In this level, the person has waded more deeply into the new Old Soul consciousness, spending two-thirds of their time in the Old Soul mindset and the other third in the Mature Soul mindset. A lot of psychological duality occurs in this stage. "Should I plunge in or not?" is a common question asked on an unconscious level. Level two Old Souls are still unsure of themselves deep down. They realize that they can function much more smoothly in the new consciousness; nevertheless, they still seek the familiar security of the old consciousness. Making a decision between comfort or maturation is the main concern of this level.

Examples: *James Taylor, J.S. Bach, Eric Clapton*

LEVEL THREE – THE "INNER INTEGRATION STAGE"

Level three Old Souls have just begun to freshly operate in the Old Soul consciousness after deciding to *take the plunge* in level two.

In a sense, level three Old Souls still have "training wheels" on, as they explore the world slowly and carefully. In this level, the Old Soul is quiet about who they are. They need a certain amount of privacy and solitude to remain balanced and in equilibrium – perhaps because they're still getting used to their new internal awakening.

Examples: *Clare Graves, Ludwig van Beethoven, Mark Twain*

LEVEL FOUR – THE "EXTERNAL INTEGRATION STAGE"

Reaching level four is like reaching a well-earned plateau after strenuous mountain climbing. In this stage, the Old Soul is a lot more confident and established in the person they are.

For this reason, the level four Old Soul tends to be more socially active and involved in the matters of the world, although at a distance.

Level four is also said to be the karmic formation level where the actions and decisions that are made determine future consequences in other levels.

Examples: *Pema Chödrön, Harrison Ford, Walt Whitman*

LEVEL FIVE – THE "DISPLACEMENT STAGE"

After adjusting to the newfound ease in level four, level five Old Souls soon begin to feel a sense of psychological and spiritual separation from the world. In other soul ages, level five signifies a period of growth towards the next level of conscious development. In the Old Soul, however, level five is accompanied by increasing feelings of detachment as everyday life, with all of its fading charms, loses its appeal. For this reason, the level five Old Soul often feels eccentric, out-of-step and unearthly. "This world is not my home," is a common sentiment felt by the level five Old Soul.

Examples: *Leonardo da Vinci, Carl Jung, Ken Keyes*

LEVEL SIX – THE "KARMA STAGE"

Level six Old Souls have managed to make peace with their feelings of "not belonging." However, in this stage they are driven to begin paying off their "karmic debts" incurred in previous levels and lifetimes. Level six is all about solving unfinished business, and for the Old Soul this emerges as a variety of trials, tribulations and tests during their lifetimes. Near the end of the level, the Old Soul is filled with a deep desire to pass on his accumulated knowledge and experience. It's not uncommon for the Old Soul to feel deeply tired and wearied by existence in this level.

Examples: *Krishnamurti, Mata Amritanandamayi (Ammachi), Thich Nhat Hanh*

LEVEL SEVEN – THE "MASTERY LEVEL"

Finally, in level seven the Old Soul can relax in retirement. However, although the seventh level Old Soul is kicking back and enjoying every moment of his earthly existence, he is still driven to pass his knowledge and wisdom on from the other 34 levels he has mastered.

The seventh level Old Soul, often referred to as the "Transcendental Soul," is likely to be a great mental or emotional counselor who understands the lessons of life in the most profound sense. Many great Spiritual Masters and Teachers were – and continue to be – seventh level Old Souls. In this stage, the Old Soul learns to flow in harmony with life again, achieving a degree of Oneness with existence. All karma has been paid off and all lessons have been learned. All that is left is deep abiding peace.

Examples: *Sri Anandamayima Ma, Ramana Maharshi, Siddhārtha Gautama*

SO ... WHY SEVEN LEVELS?

Why not four, or sixteen, or twenty-eight, or fifty-four levels? Although there isn't a whole lot of evidence supporting the soul levels theory (nor will there probably ever be), the number seven is a notoriously spiritual number.

When analyzing the world around us, the number seven mysteriously appears everywhere.

There are seven colors of the rainbow, seven planets in the solar system visible from Earth, seven days of the week, seven layers of the Earth's interior core, seven seas, seven deadly sins, seven chakras, seven continents, seven musical notes in the diatonic scale, seven days of female menstruation, seven major metals, seven major organs of the body, seven circles of hell in Islam, seven days of mourning in Judaism, seven virtues in Christianity, seven gods in Japanese mythology ... and the list goes on.

Philosopher Richard Barrett's *Levels of Consciousness* model also indicates that there are seven levels of universal inner and outer development, starting with physical survival – as in the Infant stage – and ending with spiritual service – as in the Old Soul stage.

As we can clearly see, the number seven is truly omnipresent in our lives. From biology and astronomy to music and religion, the number seven is everywhere. Perhaps the seven soul age levels are just another piece in this large, cryptic puzzle. Perhaps not.

Chapter 9

Are You a Sage or a Mystic?

»

We are all One, but then we are many. Our society is filled with a vast array of people from many different languages, colors, cultures, races, religions and personalities. It is this diversity in life which makes the world so expansive, multifaceted and enchanting.

In my time researching the Old Soul temperament, I've discovered something fascinating. Old Souls, although sharing many of the same fundamental characteristics with each other, are motivated to express themselves in two distinctly different ways. I have identified these differences as being either *thought-centered* or *emotion-centered*. Thus, I propose that there are actually *two* types of Old Souls: the "thinker" Old Soul and the "feeler" Old Soul, or in other words, the *Sage* and the *Mystic*.

TEACHING OR CREATING?

Anyone familiar with the Myer Briggs Type Indicator (MBTI) and its 16 personality types will be aware of the thinking and feeling duality in mankind.

Isabel Briggs Myers, the American researcher who created the theory in the early 20th century, popularized the idea that people either function in a predominantly logical way or in a predominantly emotional way. This widely accepted theory can be observed in the Old Soul character, which has a deep desire to self-actualize through either teaching or creating.

It's important to note that the keyword here is "predominantly." Although the Old Soul, or anyone for that matter, can be both thought and emotion-centered – desiring to both teach and create – usually one faculty is preferred over the other. Just think of our hands; we have two of them, but we choose to use one mostly over the other.

TWO TYPES OF OLD SOULS

What are the differences between the *Sage* and the *Mystic*?

Here, we'll explore both types of Old Souls and a variety of modern, historical and literary examples in each category.

I) THE SAGE

Primary Need: Teaching

TEMPERAMENT TRAITS:

- Objective, logical and thought-centered
- Decisions are made using the mind
- Problems are more linear and focused

- Neutral approach towards matters of the world (e.g., politics, religion, war, etc.)
- Steady, calm and centered
- Insightful and wise
- Philosophical and freethinking
- More likely to be lazy, apathetic and unmotivated
- Interested in philosophy, psychology and metaphysics
- *Perceive* the interconnectedness of life

Modern, Historical and Fictional Examples: Carl Jung, George Gurdjieff, Jiddu Krishnamurti, Marcus Aurelius, Diogenes, Eckhart Tolle, Zarathustra, Li Hongzhi, Thich Nhat Hanh, Lao Tzu, Ramana Maharshi, Jesus of Nazareth, Siddhartha, Mohandas Gandhi, Nikola Tesla, Socrates, Neem Karoli Baba, Abraham Lincoln

II) THE MYSTIC

Primary Need: Creation

TEMPERAMENT TRAITS:

- Intuitive, abstract and emotion-centered
- Decisions are made using the heart
- Problems are like an interconnected web
- "Go with the flow" attitude to preserve interpersonal harmony

- Empathetic and diplomatic
- Highly creative and spiritual
- More likely to be depressive and melancholic
- Interested in religion, spirituality and mysticism
- *Feel* the Oneness of life

Modern, Historical and Fictional Examples: Helena Blavatsky, Robert Frost, Emily Dickinson, Anandamayi Ma, Kahlil Gibran, Herman Melville, Paul Gaugin, Whoopie Goldberg, Alice Walker, Mattie Stepanek, Igor Stravinsky, Meryl Streep

The Sage and Mystic temperaments both share a love for solitude, and both possess highly developed introspective abilities, lack of materialistic desire, and a yearning and propensity for wisdom and truth. It would be untrue to say that one is better or smarter than the other; both have their own virtues, their own strengths and their own weaknesses.

It's also not uncommon for the Old Soul to have both Sage and Mystic traits. After all, thinking and feeling does lie on a spectrum, and very few people can ever be 100% logical or 100% emotional. Please see the *Sage and Mystic Test* at the end of the book if you're interested in discovering your type or the type of another you love.

Chapter 10

"Just Let Me Be." The Old Soul Child

»

Anne of Green Gables, Danny Delgado (*Modern Family*), Childlike Empress (*The NeverEnding Story*), Paloma Jesse (*The Hedgehog*), Ofelia (*Pan's Labyrinth*), Lucy Diamond Lawson (*I Am Sam*), Cole Sear (*The Sixth Sense*) ...

All of these fictional children show a variety of Old Soul characteristics. However, how can we determine whether *our* own children are Old Souls or not? Or whether we exhibited Old Soul characteristics as children? Also, what is the best way to raise the strange and often perplexing Old Soul child? We will explore all of these topics in this chapter, plus more.

I) CHARACTERISTICS

It's not hard to distinguish the Old Soul child from the childlike child.

As mentioned briefly at the beginning of this book, the Old Soul child is often socially maladaptive, preferring his own company or the company of adults rather than that of children his own age. Thus, the Old Soul child may appear reclusive, highly intelligent and eccentric on the outside, making it difficult for him to integrate into the social circles of his age group.

Most notably, the Old Soul child exhibits a number of key defining characteristics that sets him apart from the children around him. Often the Old Soul child:

- **Can talk easily with adults.** For instance, the Old Soul child will prefer talking to people older than him, befriending teachers at school over fellow classmates.
- **Is precocious and highly intelligent.** The Old Soul child displays an unusual mental aptitude early on in life.
- **Sounds like a "little old man" or "little old woman."** Counseling, giving advice, and interjecting wise remarks into conversations is perhaps the most notable sign of the Old Soul child.
- **Is extremely inquisitive.** Exploring, experimenting, reading books and asking incisive questions are all characteristic of the Old Soul temperament, which seeks knowledge, wisdom and truth from a young age.
- **Tends to be solitary, introverted or a "loner."** Just like in their adulthood, Old Soul children enjoy alone time and can often be

found playing by themselves. This, however, is not to be confused with shyness. Old Soul children are rarely anxious around other people, and if they are, it's usually because of parental, cultural or societal influence.

- **Are responsible.** Foolishness, carelessness and thoughtlessness are traits that are rarely attributed to the Old Soul child, who seldom has a harebrained day in his life. Instead, the Old Soul child is usually unfailingly trustworthy and adept at making thoughtful decisions.

- **Is an "underachiever" or an "overachiever."** Depending on whether the Old Soul child is more logical or more emotional, he will either excel at school work – usually to please his parents – or he will rebel against schooling – sensing the limitations of the educational system he's forced to be a student of.

II) Parenting the Old Soul Child

Although it would be ideal, there really is no one single definitive parenting blueprint for raising the Old Soul child. As with anything in life, Old Soul children are not carbon copies of each other, but each possess unique and individualized characteristics that bring exclusive and individual challenges. Thus, it's necessary to cater to the deeper nature of the Old Soul child to allow them to flourish and thrive. However, before we are able to do that, we need to first understand *what* the deeper nature of the Old Soul child in our life is like.

THE SAGE CHILD AND THE MYSTIC CHILD

What is one of the best proven ways of interacting effectively with friends, family, colleagues, and – in this case – children?

The answer: Finding out whether they use the mind or the heart to make decisions. With the Old Soul child, it's necessary to find out whether they are more of a *Sage* Old Soul or a *Mystic* Old Soul.

Below we will explore what each type of child is like. It's important to remember that children often have overlapping categories, which is precisely what makes them so precious and unique! So it's impossible to pigeonhole your child – or yourself – into any one definitive type.

THE MYSTIC CHILD

If you have a Mystic child, you will find that:

- **They are an academic overachiever.** They like to please you, they like to please their teachers, and they like to please everyone close to them because it appeals to them emotionally.
- **They tend to make friends with the teachers.** As mini adults themselves, Mystic children love listening and talking to adults. It's

not uncommon for the Mystic child to ignore his or her fellow classmates in favor of the teacher's attention.

- **Their feelings get hurt easily.** Being told off, teased or emotionally frazzled in any way takes its toll on the Mystic child. As they highly value interpersonal harmony, a breakdown in communication is both upsetting and disturbing to them. Even so, the Mystic child is not one to usually react to distressing situations with anger or rebellion, although they do prefer to spend time alone afterwards to recuperate.

- **They are gentle and empathetic.** Mystic children are often drawn to animals or other caretaking roles. It's not uncommon to see the Mystic child soothing other upset children like a father or mother, or even parenting their own parents, acting as emotional crutches in times of need.

- **They are diplomatic and cooperative.** In essence, the Mystic child wants to feel liked and they want, above all, to maintain harmony around them. For this reason, the Old Soul child may be susceptible to peer pressure and may also have difficulty in making decisions that might upset other people.

- **They enjoy giving and receiving physical affection.** The Mystic child is very demonstrative in his or her affections and loves to kiss and cuddle. It's important to remember that affection is essential to the Mystic child's well-being, especially if you're more inclined to use the mind more than the heart.

THE SAGE CHILD

The *Sage* Old Soul child, on the other hand, will exhibit a whole different set of characteristics:

- **They are likely to be academic under-achievers.** If there's anything that frustrates the precocious Sage child, it's academic rules, restrictions and syllabus. In this regard, the Sage child's favorite question is "Why?" Why learn this and not that? Why do this and be punished for that? The Sage child is more prone to seeing through the shallow nature of education, preferring instead to march to the beat of his or her own drum. After all, there is so much to learn, do, explore and discover – why be limited to the classroom! Thus, the Sage child may be misdiagnosed with disorders such as ADD or ADHD when, in fact, it is their intelligence and natural desire to amass experience and useful knowledge that gets them in trouble.

- **They are the quintessential "smart ass."** The Sage child's tongue is what gets him into a lot of trouble as a child, but it is his overactive mind which is the true culprit. Unsurprisingly, the Sage child is often mislabeled as "rebellious," "deviant" and a "smart ass," since they contradict much of what their elders dictate them to think and do, simply because it doesn't make any sense to them. It's frustrating living under parental and educational hegemony as a Sage child!

- **They're objective and assertive.** Unlike the diplomatic and cooperative Mystic child, the Sage child does not mince his words or intentions when it comes to interpersonal communication. This is because the Sage child places more importance on the facts and truth rather than on being liked or keeping the peace. Thus, the Sage child is often forthright, honest and tactless in his conversation, which can create a lot of enemies and hurt feelings. The Sage child doesn't intend to stir up controversy; rather, it is in his very nature to say things as they appear to be.

- **They're less physically affectionate.** However, they do have feelings and they require verbal and physical displays of affection just like the Mystic child in order to thrive. The Sage child shows his or her affection in a different way to the Mystic child and enjoys *doing* things to display love and affection. This could be running an errand, helping to make dinner, giving massages, or any other sign of kindness or helpfulness.

- **They enjoy giving advice.** It will be evident early on in the Sage child's life that they have a "little old man/woman" inside. Having more insight and astuteness than the average child, the Sage child will be compelled to have his or her say in matters of everyday life and will enjoy analyzing situations to discover the best possible answers. This can be disconcerting and sometimes embarrassing to the adult, or adults, on the receiving end of the Sage child's remarks. Thus, it's common for the Sage child to be labeled as a "know-it-all," "wise guy" or "smarty-pants" when they usually have a genuine, guileless interest in offering their insight.

- **They enjoy exploring and experimenting.** Accumulating information is an important part of the Sage child's youth in order to prepare for their adulthood. Reading, studying, touring and scrutinizing the surrounding environment are characteristic trademarks of the Sage child, which allow him to comprehend the world in the most thorough way. In particular, this can include probing and testing the reactions of adults in order to understand them better.

Although Sage and Mystic children possess notably different characteristics, they both share a love for solitude as well as a tendency to be thoughtful, introspective and naturally intuitive and intelligent.

III) GUIDANCE

Now that we have learned about the two distinct types of Old Soul children, what is the best way of parenting them? As mentioned previously, there really is no one definitive step-by-step model to raise the Old Soul child, as they vary so greatly in character. However, there are some important pointers to remember:

1) Give them space to be alone. The Old Soul child is naturally very reclusive. Don't force them to play with others or organize "play dates" without consulting them first.

Imposing socializing on them will burn the Old Soul child out very quickly. Alone time is necessary for them to think, to recuperate and to relax.

2) Let them have their say. No child needs authoritarian or imperious parents, especially not the Old Soul child. Show them respect and treat them as equals by allowing them to be involved in decision making, especially about their own lives. Undermining what the Old Soul child has to say by calling them names like "wise cracks," "smart asses" or "know-it-alls" will do nothing but ostracize and distance them from you.

3) Persuade and reason instead of shouting and imposing. Especially in the case of the Sage child, calm and steady reasoning is required to negotiate and agree on the reason why rules and decisions are made and enforced in the first place.

Shouting and imposing laws and regulations on the Old Soul child will do nothing but shut them off and alienate them from you.

Remember, their physical age does not represent their internal age. Rarely is the Old Soul child naïve and simple-minded in these matters.

4) Include them in conversations. Actively ask for the child's opinion. This is an excellent way of showing appreciation and esteem for who they are and what they have to say.

5) Allow them space to be themselves. Imposing your beliefs and ideas of how they "should" be only serves to impair and repress who they are. This can lead to significant emotional and psychological issues developing when the child is older. Unfortunately, many parents aren't aware of their intrusive and detrimental beliefs and perceptions when it comes to parenting a gifted child. Our current society worships "normalcy," and thus it's common for the modern-day parent to unconsciously desire his or her child to be "normal" and therefore "acceptable."

6) Value the Old Soul's rebellion as a sign of intelligence. This is a tricky one because it's not always evident what the reasons behind the Old Soul child's behavior are. Therefore, it's easy to misinterpret the child as being deliberately naughty, contradictive or impudent. Especially in the case of the Sage child, ask them for the reasons behind their cockiness or refusal to comply, and usually they will give you a reasonable answer. It's common for the Old Soul child to see through the lies, pretentions, limitations and fallacy of adult reasoning and behavior. Thus, the Old Soul child's brazenness can be seen as something valuable and even enlightening rather than devious or disobedient.

7) Show them love and affection. As with every child, the Old Soul child requires physical and verbal expressions of love to grow healthy and whole. In the case of the Sage child, praise needs to be given sincerely for a specific achievement; otherwise, it loses its legitimacy and value.

The Mystic child, on the other hand, is less logical in his or her approach and will soak up and give back as much affection as they can muster.

Remembering these simple tips and distinctions in temperament makes a world of difference in the Old Soul child's life when you allow them to live, love and become who they were destined to be from the start.

Chapter 11

Are You an Awakened Old Soul?

»

Although many Old Souls appear to be born into their temperaments, as we explored in the previous chapter, this is not always the case with every Old Soul. The truth is that many of us are born as rather plain, un-extraordinary children, and at some point during our teenage or adult years, we experience a sudden, shocking inner shift of perception. Often these spontaneous shifts of perception occur as a result of traumas such as illness, tragedy and death or major life changes like getting a new job, marrying or migrating to a different country. I refer to these shifts of perception as "awakenings" for they "wake us up" out of the everyday dream-state of living that we exist in. When we experience these awakenings, everyday life suddenly stops being so linear, narrow and predictable. Suddenly we start becoming aware of the many lies, illusions and traps inherent in the very existence we are living out, and without any warning we begin to become disillusioned and displaced from our former ways of thinking, feeling and behaving.

I am intimately acquainted with what it feels like to be an awakened Old Soul. As a child I was quite ordinary and unspectacular, and as a teenager I went through the usual periods of drama, narcissism and low self-esteem that all adolescents go through. I never expected very much from myself and I never thought I was anything more than mediocre and plain, although I was always a bit of an outcast. So for me it came as a great shock at the end of my teenage years to go through a sudden awakening process. I experienced my own awakening as a result of ruthlessly questioning my parents' fundamentalist Christian religion. Since birth I had been raised in a strict God-fearing tradition that was beginning to make less and less sense to me. Because my entire life had been built on the foundation of "this is good and this is bad; this is right and this is wrong; this is a sin and this is piety," my entire world felt as though it was being turned inside-out and upside-down. I was beginning to go through my very first experience of *la noche oscura del alma,* or "The Dark Night of the Soul" as poet and mystic Saint John of the Cross once wrote about. Little did I know that it would last for many years to come.

The Dark Night of the Soul is a phenomenon which is very closely linked to the experience of being not only an Old Soul but also a Mature Soul. As we freshly enter the alien world of The Dark Night of the Soul, it is common for us to undergo a considerable amount of emotional and psychological turbulence as we try to reconcile our authentic desires with those of the world, and as we try to distinguish the truth from the lie and the fantasy from reality. Such experiences of mental and emotional turmoil, which often results in excessive anxiety and even depression, are characteristic of the Mature Soul's newly developed self-awareness, self-discovery, and thirst for self-realization.

As we exit our old "me against the world" mentality and enter a "me working with the world" mindset, we start discovering that life isn't as black and white as we once thought. Suddenly we begin to understand that life is full of paradox, ambiguity and mystery, and suddenly we begin to realize that we aren't the center of the universe as we once thought.

Thus, at this stage of spiritual development, we begin to develop empathy for others – something that young, baby and infant souls are yet to learn.

As our discoveries about life begin to smoothly merge with our everyday waking realities, it is common for many of us to migrate from the Mature Soul mentality to the Old Soul mentality. This transitional period, which I call the "cooling off" stage, is one where we are still healing from the shock of our Mature Soul awakening, but we are beginning to make peace with what we have learned.

If you are an awakening Old Soul, you will experience the following feelings, thoughts and characteristics:

- You actively seek to empathize with people and understand life from their perspective.

- You feel a sense of social alienation as your beliefs, desires and needs don't align with the majority of people around you.

- You are beginning to understand the nature of duality – or our tendency to divide the world into either/or, us/them, good/bad extremes – and the destructive influence this has. Therefore, you adopt a more fluid "spectrum" approach to life.

- You are beginning to understand and appreciate the places that subtlety, nuance and paradox have in existence.

- You are learning how to see beyond a person's words and behaviors into the source of their pain and conditioning.

- You like exploring spiritual and philosophical thought and its relevance to life.

- You crave self-realization, or unity with truth.

- You are learning how to heal yourself from emotional and psychological trauma, finding more inner balance.

- You enjoy the little things in life and no longer feel the need to be high-maintenance.

- You understand the importance of finding and/or facilitating inner wholeness.

- You are beginning to find a sense of humor about life again.

Finally, if you are an Awakening Old Soul, you are beginning to understand the importance pain has in life, and you are beginning to welcome it and learn from it rather than trying to resist, reject or repress it. As one Old Soul by the name of Joseph wrote to me:

"I have experienced more pain than most people I know with events and circumstances that have occurred. I just feel tired and I want to go 'home.' Yet I am full of hope and feel that I have a purpose and cannot return 'home' until that purpose is completed."

This is the triumph of the Awakening Old Soul: pain no longer becomes a meaningless punishment of existence but rather a meaningful learning experience that points to a deeper purpose. Pain is inevitable, but suffering is optional.

Chapter 12

How to Deal with Loneliness, Emptiness and Disconnection as an Old Soul

»

Pain is an experience very well understood by Old Souls. Whether you have just awakened as an Old Soul, or have been one since childhood, you will more than likely experience a number of troubling and unsettling emotions. While some of these feelings may be temporary, others may haunt you as lifelong afflictions. I have narrowed down these feelings into three common categories: loneliness, emptiness and disconnection. We will explore these emotions and how to handle them in depth in this chapter.

OLD SOULS AND LONELINESS

As an Old Soul, loneliness is probably an issue for you. What happens when you do not share the same beliefs, ideologies, values, aspirations, dreams, motivations and tastes as most people in society? The result is inevitably a sense of unshakable loneliness, displacement and even melancholy. Particularly for newly awakened Old Souls, the shock of transitioning to a new level of consciousness is sometimes too difficult to handle. As old jobs, friendships, perceptions and even relationships fail to meet the new and complex needs of the Old Soul, life can appear to be barren and deserted. This sense of looming loneliness is even further amplified by the sheer scarcity of other like-minded Old Souls in our society. As a result of this perpetual feeling of isolation, it is common to feel misunderstood, rejected and even invisible or non-existent.

But where does loneliness really come from? As psychotherapist Carl Jung once wrote, "Loneliness does not come from having no people around you, but from being unable to communicate the things that seem important to you."

In this case, your loneliness as an Old Soul doesn't come from being misunderstood or misread, although that does play a supporting role in your unhappiness.

Rather, your loneliness comes from being incapable of expressing your deepest authentic self to another truly receptive person.

This means that you don't need the world to acknowledge and empathize with your needs, you just need to find an outlet of self-expression.

By nature we are social creatures. No matter how much we enjoy solitude, no matter how introverted or reclusive we may be, it is vital that we branch out and express ourselves to others. But how can we do that? How can we work to overcome the haunting feelings of loneliness that we often experience as Old Souls practically *and* productively?

This is what I have learned both personally and professionally as a transformational therapist helping others:

1. Find an outlet of self-expression. For example, consider what you are creatively passionate about. Are you interested in writing, dancing, singing, painting, sculpting or building? Think about how you can convey your thoughts, feelings and dreams through these mediums. Also, don't be afraid to limit yourself; experiment with as many creative outlets as possible to find your niche.

2. Create and prepare a simple meetup group in your local area. Like me you may be shy and somewhat bashful around new people, but don't let that hold you back. In 2011 I was suffering from chronic anxiety as a result of newly awakening as an Old Soul. Although the thought of organizing and hosting a meetup at the local bowling alley made me tremble, I knew deep down the significance of such an act and the impact it would have on my well-being and the well-being of others in the future. I'm happy to say that the bowling alley meetup was a success with about ten complete strangers from many different backgrounds showing up. Until this day I continue to stay in contact with a few of the original ten who share the same values and philosophies as me. It's amazing how one single decision can expand your life and open new remarkable doors.

The reality is that we are all hesitant about stepping outside of our comfort zones. We all get nervous and apprehensive. But if you're feeling lonely and isolated, I recommend two different approaches that may help you to connect with local, like-minded souls. Firstly, you may like to put an ad in the social section of your local newspaper including a short message, your name, and your phone number. Secondly, you may like to utilize the internet to create a local group that you can feel a sense of belonging in. At the time of writing this book, here are some useful websites and mobile apps that you may like to take a look at. While some are completely free, others require monthly membership subscriptions:

- Meetup.com (website)
- Groupspaces.com (website)
- Wegodo.com (mobile app)
- Meetme.com (mobile app)

All of these websites and apps allow you to search for people in your area and most allow you to create specialized interest groups.

An excellent way of attracting attention (and not ending up with a forlorn, empty group) is by creating multiple groups that cater to your interests. For example, you may like to create a group for local Old Souls, a group for modern philosophers, and a group for spiritual seekers. Think about what means the most to you in life, create a group, and attract people who love the same thing. Once again, this option may not be suitable, relevant or appealing to you, and that's fine. There are many other options out there.

3. Become active on social media. I'll admit that I'm not a big fan of social networks simply due to how noisy, self-promoting and overwhelming they can be, but I also realize the immense capacity they have for expanding your horizons and connecting you with other like-minded souls. This is partly why I created the "I'm an Old Soul" group on popular social networking site Facebook. Not all of the members in the Old Soul group are active, and not all of them share the same beliefs and values, but this group has connected thousands of people, many of whom have become real life friends. (There have also been a few clandestine romances!) You can find the link to the Old Soul group in the Bibliography section of this book.

Alternatively, why not create a group of your own on social media? Don't worry: if you don't know where to go or how to start a group on your app or social network of choice, a simple Google search will reveal many free and detailed guides. This may sound very obvious, but sometimes the underlying belief that "I don't know how to do this" repels us from trying in the first place. Once you know how to "do," you can act.

OLD SOULS AND EMPTINESS

The emptiness that Old Souls tend to struggle with is not a product of aimlessness or a lack of direction, as is often the case with others. Instead the Old Soul's sense of inner desolation tends to reach down to the very core of their innermost beings. This sense of profound emptiness usually comes as a direct result of experiencing "The Dark Night of the Soul," which, as I mentioned previously in the last chapter, is a period of existential angst and deep confusion about life.

As philosopher (and Old Soul) Socrates once said, "The unexamined life is not worth living."

Indeed, the deeper life is truly examined, the deeper we appear to descend into an endless night in which the essential framework that once upheld our lives seems to collapse. As all the smoke screens and illusions of life shatter and pass away, it is common for us to experience a loss of meaning and even a loss of identity.

Common symptoms of the Dark Night of the Soul include:

- Feeling as though you have come to a crossroads in life
- Becoming more conscious of your mortality
- Developing a new, alien world view
- Craving for a deeper meaning, direction or purpose in life
- Not finding value in what other's value
- Perceiving many things in life as futile
- Feeling sad, lost and alone
- No longer believing what you once believed
- Feeling like an exile or outsider in society

- Feeling as though you're living in a dark void
- Loss of identity or sense of self
- A desire for solitude
- A thirst for authenticity
- Confusion and a sense of uncertainty

As one woman from Curacao wrote to me, "I always knew that I was an Old Soul. As a kid I remembered my past life. But I feel lost in this world, alone." You may feel this haunting sensation of emptiness as well. In fact, like many Old Souls, you may have felt this emptiness for your entire life. But what can you do to resolve this feeling? Here are some of my recommendations:

1. Don't fight the abyss. Instead, allow yourself to feel empty, lonely and lost. In other words, permit yourself to fall through the void of dissolution. While this may sound like shocking advice, the reality is that resisting your feelings of emptiness actually makes them worse and amplifies them tenfold.

2. Allow yourself to feel what you feel. What is the first thing we instinctively do as human beings when we experience an uncomfortable emotion?

Naturally we run away from them, suppress them, or pretend they aren't there. Unfortunately these habits prolong our pain and deepen our suffering. The solution to this is to make a conscious habit of experiencing your emotions. When you surrender and stop fighting against the truth of what you feel, you are able to heal yourself and move on much more swiftly. But I want to quickly mention something here: it is important to remember that allowing yourself to feel your emotions is not the same as *wallowing* in them. When we wallow in our feelings we essentially romanticize them and pay excessive attention to them. Surrender isn't about self-pity, nor is it about playing the victim, but it is instead about facing what we feel with courage and then quickly moving on.

But what happens when our emotions are chronic and persistent? Sometimes persistent emotions can be faced and released quickly, but other times they can't. ... What do we do then?

3. Have faith and trust that life will unfold exactly as it's meant to.

The reality is that we only perceive a very tiny fraction of what can be perceived. We only understand a very small percentage of what can be understood. The beauty of life is that it is a mystery, and this Mystery also has its own innate wisdom. Whether we like to call this wisdom God, Consciousness or Divinity, the truth is that many of the toughest experiences in life forge the strongest and deepest souls. Often pain is a precursor to joy, abundance and enlightenment. When we give our pain a purpose, it ceases to rip apart our lives.

4. Find something that gives you meaning or a sense of fulfillment. One of the best ways to remedy,

or at least soothe the feeling of inner emptiness, is to explore self-actualization. For example, you may like to examine the following questions:

- What dreams, aspirations and desires have you left unfulfilled in life?
- What did you envision yourself doing when you were younger that you later forgot?
- What unexplored paths have you left untraveled which seem daunting?

Answering these questions may reveal a lot about what you find meaning in and how you can cultivate more inner fulfillment in your life. Even finding purpose in *having no* purpose is a worthy way of creating inner calm and wholeness. At the end of the day, what is more enjoyable than purely experiencing the present moment with all its small joys and wonders? Often the simplest and most breathtaking pleasures in life are right in front of us, in this very moment.

OLD SOULS AND DISCONNECTION

When the 16th century poet and mystic Saint John of the Cross wrote about the Dark Night of the Soul, he explored the misery and desolation one feels when experiencing the tribulations of life that separate one from God. Such a profound sense of disconnection with the Divine is a sensation sometimes felt by Old

Souls, and frequently experienced by those freshly entering this stage of consciousness.

As the burdens, struggles and tragedies of the world begin to weigh down on the Old Soul, the point of living life is questioned. Suddenly the dimmest and most enigmatic questions are asked and pursued exhaustively. "Why do good people suffer?" "What is the meaning of life?" "What happens after we die?" As life, with all its apparent senselessness is examined through new eyes, an endless barrage of questions arise, many of which can never quite be answered sufficiently.

"Why was I even born in the first place?" This question marks a period of desperation and emotional exhaustion in the Old Soul's quest for answers. Eventually, the feeling of disconnection felt towards the Holiness of life hollows into a form of existential depression and quiet despair.

I am very well acquainted with what it's like to experience disconnection from Spirit. I know how painful it can be to feel lost and abandoned in life. I have also witnessed the varying effects that this feeling has had on other people's lives.

While I don't have all the answers, I have discovered a number of extremely useful things on my path which may help you if you struggle with this problem. You are welcome to accept or reject as many of these suggestions as you like. At the end of the day, listen to *your own* truth.

1. **Give yourself the permission to disconnected.** The moment we feel lost or cut off have a tendency to run and hide. We don't want to experience such painful emotions, and yet, by stopping and allowing ourselves to feel lost and incomplete, we paradoxically feel much more whole. Why is this the case? The answer is that when we stop resisting and fighting against what we feel, we mentally and emotionally relax. This relaxation helps to ground us in the present moment rather than in thoughts and feelings of what was or what could be.

2. **Investigate the questions you ask about life.** I have often found that our questions about life tend to be biased, colored and distorted due to our long-held beliefs, ideals, assumptions and misconceptions.

When we closely examine the questions we ask about existence, it is common for us to gain a lot of unexpected clarity and insight. Famous physician and author Edward de Bono referred to this as "lateral thinking" which is a form of reasoning that involves approaching problems from different angles. For example, you might like to take the question, "What is the meaning of life?" and instead ask, "Why *should* life have a meaning?" I recommend Roger von Oech's book "A Whack on the Side of the Head: How You Can Be More Creative" as a source of inspiration for unconventional thinking tips.

3. **Learn to find happiness again in the present moment.** After all, the more we look here and there

appease our restless minds, the more we ... th the joy that can be found right here, in ... moment. Happiness and fulfillment cannot ... overed in future accomplishments or ...ations.

Have you ever noticed that the second you attain what you've been striving for, you immediately want more? Isn't that ironic? We spend our entire lives believing that if we buy this, do that, don't do this, go there, we will finally have joy and peace. But the very act of searching, craving and looking obscures the truth of this very moment, that is, happiness and peace exist right *now*. God, the Tao, Consciousness, Source, Divinity, Life and Love can be experienced right now regardless of how many answers you do or don't have, how great your life is or what you've done to deserve it. The Buddhist's call this taste of divine Presence, "Samadhi." If this concept confuses you, or you would like to learn more, I recommend looking into the writings of teachers such as Ramana Maharshi, Adyashanti, Gangaji, Scott Kiloby and Sri Nisargadatta Maharaj to expand your understanding.

4. Spend at least twenty minutes every day in solitude. As an Old Soul you will already experience a pull towards alone time, but sometimes your daily duties and responsibilities may engulf your life.

Solitude gives us the space to become aware of how we are feeling and how to enjoy the simplicity of Being. You may like to spend your alone time simply allowing yourself to experience and observe the many emotions and thoughts that rise within you (similar to a meditation practice). Or you may like to sit in quiet reflection observing the interrelatedness and ultimate Oneness of everything. Regardless of how you decide to spend your time, a daily practice of solitude is immensely beneficial to your well-being.

Chapter 13

What Do Life, Death, Truth and Love Really Mean?

»

Now that we have dealt with the practical and emotional elements of the Old Soul temperament, it is time for us to delve into the philosophical elements intrinsic to the Old Soul's way of perceiving the world.

During the process of writing this book, I was fortunate enough to have received a number of personal reflections from Old Souls all over the world detailing their thoughts, feelings and beliefs about birth, death, and everything in between.

In this chapter, we will explore a small collection of deeply inspiring and thought-provoking reflections from real-life Old Souls on four of the most significant and meaningful topics of existence: life, death, truth and love.

While life, death, truth and love all mean something slightly different to each one of us, the remarkable thing about the following reflections is that they all share a very similar vibe. I will leave you to discover what that is.

> "Truth to me is what's spoken within but can't be said. Life is the end. Death is the beginning."
> – Friedolf Pierrot, Netherlands

> "Truth to me is an eternal mystery, always revealing itself in new and magnificent ways. Life to me is sacred. Death to me is a release, the greatest mystery, the ultimate initiation into yourself. Love to me is all there ever is." – Vanja Bjørke, Norway

> "Truth to me is knowledge, life to me is experience, death to me is liberation and love is the ultimate goal." – Aishwarya More, India

> "Life is the most beautiful mystery. It's the realization of the universe through living things, through consciousness." – Olivier Rouquette, France

> "Truth is love, love is truth, nothing else matters. Life is learning, and death, as we call it, is only a door to our 'real' life." – Beverly Janson, Tennessee, USA

> "Love to me is the base, the energy of the

Universe. It connects everything, it gives meaning to everything, it Is." – Bea Agudo, Spain

"Truth to me is knowing. Life to me is meaningless without truth. Death is the next step in our journey of the truth. Love is the ultimate sacrifice; the sacred sharing of one's self." – Luann McDonnell, Arizona, USA

"Truth changes from person to person and situation to situation, but still there remains truth. Life is an indefinite rollercoaster ride of emotions and experiences, but is worth embarking on. Love brings life in harmony; it connects us to soul, self and others." – Rome Nimkar, India

"Truth is the only thing that can bring us closer to god/consciousness. It is only through challenging our beliefs that we can reach truth. Love is the basic principle which gives birth to every other principle such as truth, courage, empathy, freedom and growth." – Mudit Gupta, India

"Death to me is an inescapable liberation from the entrapment of self. Love to me is acceptance of what is. Love is not picking the blossoming flower; love is letting the flower be alive with you in the present." – Imani Danzy, USA

"Love is perfection. It is the reason, the meaning, the truth that makes us who we are."
– Stancho Stanchev, Bulgaria

Chapter 14

"Old Souls Don't Identify With Labels." Exploring the Transcendental Soul

»

The title of this chapter reveals a very interesting observation made by quite a few people I have spoken with during my research. The argument sounds something like this:

If Old Souls see through the fallacy of the ego, why do they feel the need to identify with a label?

Or as one person commented in response to an online question I asked about the meaning of being an "Old Soul":

"To me, this 'old soul' notion is just another concept people have invented to make them feel better about themselves. It is ego crawling through the backdoor."

Such an observation is immensely useful to our growth as spiritual beings having a human experience. After all, isn't our identification with the idea of being an Old Soul yet another illusion of the ego? Isn't our fixation with such a label preventing us from tasting the nectar of our true nature which is not composed of thoughts, feelings, words, beliefs and sensations that change, evolve and decay – but instead consists of a radiant, changeless and eternal wholeness?

Isn't it true that at the core of "who we are" lives an ever-present purity of being that is not influenced by any thought-form, whether good or bad?

Although identifying as an Old Soul can prevent us from experiencing this reality, it can also paradoxically help us draw nearer to this reality through the process of self-understanding and acceptance.

After all, how can we overcome the ego without first building one? How can we ever transcend our limited sense of self without first developing a well-formed sense of self? For this reason, it is essential that we learn to understand who we think we are and to realize that we are not alone in our deepest needs and longings.

If anything, that is the true value of identifying with the label "Old Soul" on our paths of inner growth: finally we can give a name to what we feel and desire at our deepest level.

But the journey doesn't just end there. There comes a time when such a form of identification evolves from being a type of liberation to being a type of entrapment. There comes a time when it is necessary to shed this label after it has served its purpose. At this point, in order to truly merge with our essential nature, it is important for us to progressively release all labels, all beliefs, all assumptions and all stories of who we think we are in order to experience the true depths of liberation. This is what is referred to as the "Transcendental Soul," but the one experiencing such bliss does not go by any label for that would be to return again to the divisive traps of the mind rather than to embrace the limitless Oneness inherent in all existence.

Becoming a "transcendental being" can be thought of as the ultimate destination the Old Soul is traveling towards in the journey of their life.

Conclusion

»

Poet and novelist Charles Bukowski once wrote, "My heart is a thousand years old. I am not like other people." His words perfectly encapsulate what it means to be an Old Soul – something that this book has explored at length. From uncovering how the Old Soul feels about life, death, love, family, religion and truth to expounding on current theories and classifications that explain the phenomenon of feeling old inside, we have navigated through many themes in this book that I hope have greatly enriched your understanding of what it means to feel old at heart.

As we come to our final leg of this journey, my greatest wish is that this book continues to help you on your own personal journey of self-understanding, and I hope that it has assisted you to better understand the people around you more wholly and compassionately. Awareness and understanding, after all, form the cornerstones of compassion, empathy and love.

May this voyage into the mysterious world of Old Souls continue to help you embrace and appreciate your own gifts and unique value – as well as those of others – in this large and often alienating world.

Appendix

Are you an Old Soul? The following test will allow you to explore your level of soulful maturity firsthand. At the end of the test, your answers will reveal whether you are most likely an Old Soul, Mature Soul, Younger Soul, or transitional Soul who is in the process of moving from one Soul Age to another. Please answer each question honestly. If you find it hard to answer any particular question, please select "Undecided."

I recommend that you take some time to mark or highlight your answers to this test using a pen or pencil (if you wish). This will help you to easily track your answers at the end.

ARE YOU AN OLD SOUL?

1. Before making a decision:

a) I reflect on any future consequences.

b) I consider how the decision will make me feel in the present moment.

c) I consider how the decision will make me look.

d) Undecided.

2. When I am in a group of people, I am like:

a) The mother, father, or confidant.

b) The friend or comforter.

c) The acquaintance that shares interesting trivia and gossip.

d) Undecided.

3. People tend to perceive me as:

a) An outsider, "hippie," or "kook."

b) A delicate and sensitive person.

c) One of them.

d) Undecided.

4. When trying to solve problems, I tend to:

a) Approach the issue from a bird's eye perspective.

b) Approach the issue from a detail-orientated perspective.

c) Try to discover who is to blame.

d) Undecided.

5. Which of the following statements is true for you?

a) I am comfortable with being thought of as weird and unacceptable.

b) I am uncomfortable with being thought of as weird and unacceptable – but I wish I was comfortable with it.

c) I could not tolerate being thought of as weird or unacceptable.

d) Undecided.

6. Most of my friends:

a) Are older than me.

b) Are the same age as me.

c) Are the same age or younger than me.

d) Undecided.

7. Which of the following statements is true for you?

a) Nature inspires and invigorates me.

b) Nature calms my nerves.

c) Nature is nice, but it isn't really a big part of my life right now.

d) Undecided.

8. When witnessing scenes of suffering, I often:

a) Become reflective, introspective and saddened.

b) Become deeply disturbed and depressed.

c) Become infuriated or attempt to block my uncomfortable feelings out.

d) Undecided.

9. Which of the following statements is true for you?

a) I feel deeply, but I rarely become possessed or controlled by my emotions.

b) I feel deeply, and I sometimes become possessed or controlled by my emotions.

c) I feel deeply, and I frequently become possessed or controlled by my emotions.

d) Undecided.

10. People have frequently described me as:

a) Insightful and wise.

b) Perceptive and diplomatic.

c) Entertaining and outgoing.

d) Undecided.

11. Having a successful career to me:

a) Is unimportant.

b) Is important.

c) Is vital.

d) Undecided.

12. Which of the following statements is true for you?

a) I feel as though I have more life experience than my age reflects.

b) I feel as though life is constantly throwing curveballs my way which I often struggle to deal with.

c) I frequently feel scared, confused, intimidated and lost in life.

d) Undecided.

13. In life I value:

a) Truth, freedom and understanding.

b) Meaning and connection.

c) Comfort, success and security.

d) Undecided.

14. My judgments about people are:

a) Almost always correct and confirmed.

b) Often correct and sometimes confirmed.

c) Sometimes correct.

d) Undecided.

15. In solitude I feel:

a) Whole, complete and happy.

b) Relieved, but sometimes lonely.

c) Uncomfortable, incomplete and restless.

d) Undecided.

16. To me, joy can be found:

a) In the little things, at any time.

b) When life is peaceful.

c) When I am successful, liked and valued.

d) Undecided.

17. Which of the following statements is true for you?

a) I respect tradition, but I consider myself to be more of a liberal person.

b) I fluctuate between conservative and liberal values.

c) I am very conservative.

d) Undecided.

18. When challenges arise:

a) I value them as opportunities to grow or learn.

b) I feel depressed or anxious.

c) I get angry.

d) Undecided.

19. When someone deliberately hurts me:

a) I try to understand the reason why, without taking it personally.

b) I become extremely upset and take it personally.

c) I try to hurt them back to teach them a lesson.

d) Undecided.

20. Which of the following issues are you more prone to experiencing?

a) Existential depression.

b) Anxiety disorders such as social anxiety, general anxiety, and OCD.

c) Addiction (e.g. drugs, alcohol, sex, gambling, etc.).

d) Undecided.

Tally your results.

If you chose **mostly (a)**, you display Old Soul characteristics.

If you chose **mostly (b)**, you display Mature Soul characteristics.

If you chose **mostly (c)**, you display a mixture of Infant, Baby, and Young Soul characteristics.

If you chose **mostly (d)**, you might be transitioning between one Soul Age to another. For example, you might be a Mature Soul who is shifting to the Old Soul's level of consciousness, or a Young Soul who is shifting to the Mature Soul's level of consciousness, and so forth.

Sage and Mystic Test

Take the following test to determine whether you are primarily a feeling or thinking centered Old Soul. If you find it hard to select one definitive answer, please select "Undecided."

1. Which of the following statements is true for you?
a) The world often tires me.
b) The world often depresses me.
c) Undecided.

2. When someone comes to me with a problem:
a) I try to fix it.
b) I offer immediate emotional support.
c) Undecided.

3. When I have to make a decision in life:
a) I think through the consequences very deeply.

b) I go with my gut instinct.

c) Undecided.

4) Which of the following statements is true for you?

a) The sciences and philosophy attract me.

b) The arts and spirituality attract me.

c) Undecided.

5) Peer pressure:

a) Doesn't affect me.

b) Does affect me.

c) Undecided.

6) I am prone to being:

a) Lazy and apathetic.

b) Depressed and melancholic.

c) Undecided.

7) Which of the following statements is true for you?

a) Arguments don't bother me.

b) Arguments unsettle me.

c) Undecided.

8) More than anything, I love to:

a) Teach people what I know.

b) Create something of significance and beauty.

c) Undecided.

9) I express my emotions:

a) Through actions more than through words.

b) Through words more than through actions.

c) Undecided.

10) I am fascinated more by:

a) The paradoxes and riddles of life.

b) The beauty and profound mystery of life.

c) Undecided.

11) Which of the following statements is true for you?

a) I would make a good professor or scholar.

b) I would make a good healer or counselor.

c) Undecided.

12) I read books:

a) To gain knowledge.

b) To gain pleasure.

c) Undecided.

13. Which of the following statements is true for you?

a) When I speak I try to be pragmatic and clear.

b) When I speak I try to be diplomatic and understanding.

c) Undecided.

14. Emotionally, I have a:

a) Thick skin.

b) Thin skin.

c) Undecided.

15. Which of the following statements is true for you?

a) Truth is my driving force.

b) Love is my driving force.

c) Undecided.

Tally your results.

If you chose **mostly (a)**, you display **Sage** characteristics. As a logical, philosophical and freethinking person, your primary need is to teach.

If you chose **mostly (b)**, you display **Mystic** characteristics. As an artistic, intuitive and abstract person, your primary need is to create.

If you chose **mostly (c)**, or a mixture of (a) and (b), it is likely that you display **both Sage and Mystic** characteristics. As a person who shares both thinking and feeling traits, your primary need is to mentor others.

Bibliography

Barrett, R. (2010). *The new leadership paradigm*. Retrieved from Lulu.com

Bowman, C. (1997). *Children's past lives: How past life memories affect your child*. New York: Bantam Books.

Carvajal, D. (2012). *On the trail of inherited memories*. Retrieved September 24, 2013, from http://www.reincarnationexperiment.org/images/ RC_REXP_DNA_Memory_.pdf

Dexter, N. (2011). *Past life regression*. Retrieved September, 27, 2013, from http://www.nicoladexter.com/html/ therapies/pastlife.php

Facebook. (2015). *I'm an old soul.* Retrieved June 23, 2015, from https://www.facebook.com/groups/ imanoldsoul

Harvey, K. (2012). *Is your child ruled by logic or emotion?* Retrieved October 2, 2013, from http://www.clarityandbalance.com/2009/ is-your-child-ruled-by-logic-or-emotion.html

Hoodwin, S. (n.d.). *Celebrity overleaves*. Retrieved September 14, 2013, from http://www.michaelteachings.com/ celebrities-by-roles.html

Jax-Castillo, C. (2009). *How to raise a "Dakota Fanning".* Retrieved October 1, 2013, from http://www.soulscode.com/ is-there-a-dakota-fanning-in-your-family/

Maslow, A.H. (1943). A theory of human motivation. *Psychological Review, 50* (4), 370-396.

Maslow, A.H. (1970). *Motivation and personality.* New York: Harper & Row.

McGuinness, B. (2012). *Reincarnation: the 35 steps of soul evolution.* Retrieved September 12, 2013, from http://personalityspirituality.net/articles/the-michael-teachings/reincarnation-the-35-steps/

Michael Education Foundation. (n.d.). *Soul perception on the physical plane.* Retrieved September 7, 2013, from http://www.michaeleducationalfoundation.com/michael-system-basics/overview-of-the-michael-teaching/soul-perception-on-the-physical-plane

Myers, I.B. (1995). *Gifts differing: Understanding personality type.* Palo Alto: Davies-Black Publishing.

O'Mahony, E. (2013). *How epigenetics is dissolving the lines between science and spirituality.* Retrieved September 22, 2013, from http://consciouslifenews.com/epigenetics-dissolving-lines-between-science-spirituality/1159387/

Sol, D.M. (2014). *Soulful energy: Origins of the soul.* Retrieved June 29, 2015, from http://lonerwolf.com/soulful-energy/

Wheeler, M. (2009). *Study gives more proof that intelligence is largely inherited.* Retrieved September 5, 2013, from http://newsroom.ucla.edu/portal/ucla/more-proof-that-intelligence-is-85134.aspx

Wittmeyer, P. (n.d.). *The old soul.* Retrieved August 15, 2013, from http://www.michaelteachings.com/old_soul.html

About the Author

Aletheia Luna is the author and co-founder of the popular self-discovery website lonerwolf.com, where she has authored hundreds of unique articles and tests on a host of subjects ranging from psychology and sociology to self-improvement and spirituality since 2012. As a modern mystic, transformational mentor and holistic writer, she has guided thousands of people all throughout the world on their paths to self-acceptance and wholeness. She is an introvert and an Old Soul at heart, and is the co-creator and administrator of the "I'm an Old Soul" online group, which to date consists of over 10,000 self-identified Old Souls. She is presently living in Perth, Western Australia, and *Old Souls* is her first book.

For questions, comments or suggestions, please feel free to send her an email at: luna@lonerwolf.com.

If you would like to discuss this book or talk to other Old Souls, you can join the Old Soul Facebook group here: www.facebook.com/groups/imanoldsoul/

If you enjoyed reading this book, please feel free to share your thoughts and opinions on www.goodreads.com or www.amazon.com.

»

Other Books by Aletheia Luna

Quiet Strength: Embracing, Empowering and Honoring Yourself as an Introvert

Written for the quiet people of life, transformational mentor and holistic writer Aletheia Luna takes us on an inspiring journey of self-rediscovery and empowerment, asserting that it is not necessary to change who we are or to fight our reserved natures to live fulfilling lives as introverts. Written with compassion and insight, *Quiet Strength* takes us on six powerful paths to quiet vitality.

Printed in Great Britain
by Amazon